GRAPHIC BY MICHELANGELO
[SUPPOSITITIOUSLY TITLED]

The True Purpose of Man

MICHAEL Q. SIEVERSON

with

J. BARTHOLOMEW WALKER

Quadrakoff Publications Group, LLC
Wilmington, Delaware
USA

Copyright © 2020 Quadrakoff Publications Group, LLC All rights reserved.

Except as noted, All NASB scriptures taken from The New American Standard Bible® Copyright © 1960, 1962, 1963, 1968, 1971, 1972, 1973, 1975, 1977, 1995 by the Lockman Foundation, LaHabra, CA. Special thanks to the Lockman Foundation for the finest Bible version available; as well as for their permission to use the same. All Scripture passages taken from The Holy Bible, King James Version, are as noted.

ISBN: 978-1-948219-73-0

All rights reserved. No part of this publication may be reproduced, stored in a retrieval system or transmitted, in any form, or by any means, electronic, mechanical, recorded, photocopied, or otherwise, without the prior written permission of both the copyright owner and the above publisher of this book, except by a reviewer who may quote brief passages in a review.

The scanning, uploading, and distribution of this book via the Internet or via any other means without the permission of the publisher is illegal and punishable by law. Please purchase only authorized electronic editions and do not participate in or encourage electronic piracy of copyrightable materials. Your support of the author's rights is appreciated.

Any and all characters appearing that are not in any of the versions of the Bible are fictional. Any resemblance to any living person is strictly coincidental.

Contains some previously published material, which can be found in other QPG publications.

Printed in the United States of America.

The True Purpose of Man

It would be so easy to say that the answer to the question: "What is the true purpose of man?" depends upon precisely whom it is that is asked. But of course, this cannot be so. There can be only one true answer as to the purpose of man; and that is that *actual* purpose or purposes for which God Himself *created* man.

Different religions proffer various ideas regarding this. Some claim that the purpose of the earth is a place for man to live for eternity in bliss. Perhaps this is so, but it must be asked from precisely where this idea was derived.

The True Purpose of Man

Secular sources have various different viewpoints ranging from: "dying with the most toys," to theories that make even less sense.

The "man" occupied world has spent much of its time in substantial misery—at least with regard to the condition of man. And this condition of man often provides the fodder for many to question the existence of God; and/or His nature. After all, with the various messes the earth has been in for so much of the time, who needs a God? "I can mess things up my self—thank you very much. I don't need any help."

So precisely when and how did all of this start? If it can be stipulated that the Bible may have something of value to say about this matter; then perhaps some knowledge and subsequent wisdom can be attained.

The Bible tells us it all started: "In the beginning." Genesis 1:1 (KJV) tells us:

> *"In the beginning God created the heaven and the earth."*[1]

Precisely what is this "in the beginning?"

The actual original Hebrew word translated as: "*in the beginning*" is:

> "7225 rê'shîyth; from the same as 7218; the first, in place, time, order or rank (spec. a firstfruit)...."[2]

In order to have any type of *sequencing*, such as "the first," there must be *time*. Science tells us of the

"Big Bang;" before which there was no time, no space, and no matter. Thus when this event occurred, (Big Bang); this represented the bringing into existence of the three, (time, space, and matter); or the bringing into existence of the *material* realm.

Thus if it is stipulated that the word "*heaven*" here in Genesis 1:1 cannot be the same "heaven" God "art in;" by Hobson's choice, this "*heaven*" must refer to the space in the *material* realm. In addition, God could not have resided in a yet to be created realm before He created the same.

So there was initially by definition an *immaterial* realm, with no time, space, or matter; and necessarily from that realm, God created a (*material*) realm, with time, space, and matter. Thus Genesis 1:1, and the "Big Bang;" represent the very same event.

What type of matter did God utilize in creating the material realm? The answer is none, because no matter existed prior to the creation of matter. Thus God did not *form*, *fashion*, or *mold* the material realm from matter, He *created* it.

The actual Hebrew word translated here as "created" is:

> "1254 bârâ', a prim. root; (absol.) to create; (qualified) to cut down (a wood), select, feed (as formative processes): - choose, create (creator), cut down, dispatch, do, make (fat)."[3] "The verb expresses creation out of nothing..."[4]

The True Purpose of Man

And we are told that the creation of the earth was completed at the end of Genesis 1:1.

But the beginning of the very next verse and onward, tells us of an entirely different situation.

Genesis 1:2 (KJV) tells us:

> *"And the earth was without form,*
> *and void; and darkness was upon*
> *the face of the deep.*
> *And the Spirit of God moved*
> *upon the face of the waters."*[5]

The Interlinear Bible states: "she became;"[6] thus indicating a change from the conclusion of Genesis 1:1. Thus in continuous form this would read: "*In the beginning God created the heaven and the earth,*" and "*she became,*" (after earth's creation was completed), *without form* and *void.*"

In order to better understand what took place here; and most particularly man's future role in the same; it would be prudent to bypass what God Himself began doing at that time, and "jump ahead" to the entrance of man on to the scene. [For a full analysis of God's actions *before* creating man see: "*MeekRaker Beginnings...*"]

Genesis 1:26 (KJV) tells us:

> *"And God said, Let us make man*
> *in our image, after our likeness:*
> *and let them have dominion*
> *over the fish of the sea,*
> *and over the fowl of the air,*
> *and over the cattle, and over all the*

The True Purpose of Man

> *earth, and over every creeping thing
> that creepeth upon the earth."*[7]

Here in Genesis 1:26, God "announces" His intentions, and the very next verse, tells us what God in fact did.

Genesis 1:27 (KJV) tells us:

> *"So God created man in his own image,
> in the image of God created he him;
> male and female created he them."*[8]

After first *announcing* His intentions, including His intention to grant man "*dominion;*" God then *created* man: "*in his own image,*" and in the "*image of God.*" Here we are *twice* told precisely whom it was that man "took after"—lest anyone in the future claiming to represent God or otherwise, suggest differently.

The actual original Hebrew word translated as "have dominion" in verse 26 is:

> "7287 râdâh; a prim. root; to *tread* down, i.e. *subjugate*; spec. to *crumble* off: - (come to, make to) have dominion, prevail against..."[9]

And we are then *three* times told in verse 27, precisely *how* it was that God brought man into existence: "*God created man,*" "*God created he him,*" and "*male and female created he them.*" It seems that God wanted to be sure all knew precisely *how* these "created creatures" were brought into existence—lest anyone in the future claiming to represent God or otherwise, *confuse* this with another event, which they did, (would *later* do).

So what is or are, the word or words, translated as "*created*" three times in this verse."

The actual Hebrew word appearing three times, and *translated* three times as "*created;*" is the aforementioned *bârâ'*.[10]

When God *created* the *material* realm, with time, space, and matter; this was *bârâ'*. There was nothing *material* utilized, as there was nothing *material* yet in existence *to* utilize.

Here when God *created* man, it is likewise *bârâ'*. But unlike when He *created* the *material* realm, here; although God *could* have utilized *matter* in causing man to come into existence, as matter *did* exist at this time; He did not—at least not for the events described in *these* passages.

In the very next verse, God then "charges," created man; telling them *collectively*, precisely what it is He wants them to do. Thus that which is contained therein, represents God's primary will with regard to man.

Genesis 1:28 (KJV) tells us:

> "And God blessed them,
> and God said unto them,
> Be fruitful, and multiply,
> and replenish the earth, and subdue it:
> and have dominion over the fish of
> the sea, and over the fowl of the air,
> and over every living thing
> that moveth upon the earth."[11]

The True Purpose of Man

This seems a rather peculiar thing for God to do, given that He is *omniscient*, *omnipotent*, and *omnipresent*. If as many believe, the earth was not actually completed at the end of Genesis 1:1, despite what we are literally told; "subdue" seems a strange request or order by God, for man's assistance in the completion of the same.

Some believe that God sends us "challenges" to make us "better;" and likely some would try to proffer Genesis 1:28 in furtherance of this theory. But there is that pesky: "*in his own image,*" and in the "*image of God,*" part.

It is also unclear how a perfect being could be capable of creating any imperfection. Stated differently, precisely how could any *subset* of the *set* "perfect," contain that which is imperfect.

And finally, if this: "challenges in order to improve" theory had any factual basis; then it seems there would be some commonality between some actions of God, and some actions of Satan.

This "*subdue*" part, is especially problematic, given the actual Hebrew word *translated* here as "*subdue.*"

This actual Hebrew word translated here as "subdue" is:

> "3533 kâbash; a prim. root; to *tread* down; hence neg. to *disregard*; pos. to *conquer*, *subjugate*, *violate*: - bring into bondage, force, keep under, subdue, bring into subjection."[12]

The "*it*" in "*and subdue it,*" contextually clearly refers to the *earth*. Thus God's will with regard to man is to: "to *tread* down" and "*conquer, subjugate, violate*" the earth. The English word *kibosh*, as in: "put the kibosh on it," is derived from the Hebrew *kâbash*.

So it must be asked as to why God would create a world that was so imperfect, that He later had to create man in order to finish the job for him? The answer is that He did not do so; and likely could not have done so.

Although examining precisely what happened between Genesis 1:1 and Genesis 1:2, that caused the earth to require *kâbash*; is beyond the scope of this work; (See "*Ostium Ab Inferno*"); it should be asked if there is any other evidence to support that that which is contained in the above Genesis 1:28, is in fact how it reasonably reads.

Genesis 2:1 tells us:

> "*Thus the heavens and the earth were finished, and all the host of them.*"[13]

There are two statements that are made here: "*Thus the heavens and the earth were finished,*" and: "*and all the host of them.*" These should each be addressed separately.

With regard to: "*the heavens and the earth were finished,*" the actual Hebrew word translated as "finished" is:

> "3615 kâlâh; a prim. root; to *end*, whether intrans. (to *cease, be finished, perish*) or trans. (to *complete, prepare, consume*)..."[14]

The True Purpose of Man

It would be easy to simply say: "See, the earth wasn't finished until Genesis 2:1." But *"finished"* or *kâlâh*, can refer to *any* type of *process* or *processes*. Here in Genesis 2:1, it is *both* the *"heavens and the earth;" "and,"* (not "or"); *"the host of them"* that we are told were *"finished,"* or *kâlâh*. Thus this statement could not have been true, until that which took place in Genesis 1:27, (the creation of man), had also been *"finished."*

No one argues that God "did a bunch of stuff," after Genesis 1:1; and the passages that immediately follow Genesis 2:1, provide some insight into this in the very *general* sense.

The verses immediately following Genesis 2:1, here Genesis 2:2-4, (KJV) tell us:

"And on the seventh day
God ended his work which he had made;
and he rested on the seventh day
from all his work which he had made.

And God blessed the seventh day,
and sanctified it: because that in it he
had rested from all his work which
God created and made.

These are the generations of the heavens
and of the earth when they were created,
in the day that the Lord God made
the earth and the heavens,"[15]

In Genesis 2:2, the word *"made"* appears twice.

The True Purpose of Man

In Genesis 2:3, the words "*created*" and "*made*" each appear once.

In Genesis 2:4, the words "*created*" and "*made*" each appear once.

It must be asked why these two different words appear? Culinary novices often will state they *made* something; but when the result is dubious, it is often then referred to as their *creation*.

The original Hebrew word translated as "made" each time is:

> "6213 'âsâh; a prim. root; to do or make, in the broadest sense and widest application..."[16]

The original Hebrew word translated as "created" each time is the aforementioned 1254 *bârâ'*.[17]

In the case of *'âsâh*, this could refer to anything *made*: "in the broadest sense and widest application..." Thus *bârâ'* could technically fit into the definition of *'âsâh*.

But although *bârâ'* could technically fit into the definition of *'âsâh*; not all *'âsâh* is *bârâ'*.

Meaning that: "to do or make, in the broadest sense and widest application...;" includes *all* means of "making," whether *matter* was utilized or was not. But *bârâ'* requires that *nothing* material be utilized— as in the creation of the universe, where as previously stated, there was no matter available at that "time" to be used.

Thus with regard to these passages, it seems that distinctions are being made with respect to whether or not matter could have been utilized in the process. When the translation as "*created*," (bârâ'),

The True Purpose of Man

appears; this *precludes* the use of matter. When the translation as "*made*," ('âsâh), appears; this generally includes the use of matter, but also does not necessarily preclude *bârâ'*.

Therefore, it seems reasonable that since *both* of these words appear in these passages; "*made*," as *'âsâh*; likely refers to the use of matter in the process; and "*created*," as *bârâ'*; likely refers to a process where matter was not utilized.

So it must be asked precisely what it is we are told was "finished" when we are told in Genesis 2:1: "*Thus the heavens and the earth were finished*," and: "*and all the host of them.*" [It should be noted that at this point in time, Adam had yet to be *formed*.]

There are *three* distinct things under discussion in these verses. The first is the *creation*, or *bârâ'* of the heavens and the earth. The second in whatever God "*made*," or *'âsâh* . And the third is the *creation*, or *bârâ'* of man. Thus it seems what was "*finished*," includes all three; and not just the *creation*, or *bârâ'* of the heavens and the earth.

And as will be seen, the "*finished*" is from God's perspective and role only; and not from the perspective of the final product; i.e.; the condition of the earth at that time.

In verse 2 we are told "*And on the seventh day God ended his work which he had made; and he rested on the seventh day from all his work which he had made.*" This passage literally refers to only what God "*made;*" and not what He "*created*"—something which is then confirmed in verse 3.

Verse 3 tells us: "*And God blessed the seventh day, and sanctified it: because that in it he had rested from all his work which God created and made."* Here the distinction is made, by the inclusion of both *"created"* and *"made."*

But does this make any degree sense? We are told here that God *"blessed"* and *"sanctified"* the *"seventh day;" "because"* He *"rested."*

A word about the translation as: *"day."* Most believe that the use of *"day"* here; represents a *literal* twenty four hour day. However, the word "day" can also relate to a period of *activity*, (*chiros*); as well as a fixed period of *time*, (*kronos* or *chronos*).

The actual Hebrew word translated as "day" is:

> "3117 yôwm; from an unused root mean. to *be hot*; a *day* (as the *warm* hours), whether lit. (from sunrise to sunset, or from one sunset to the next), or fig. (a space of time defined by an associated term), [often used adv.]..."[18]

Thus it could be the case that this "rested," likely signified the end of the period of *activity*, rather than the twenty four hour *"day."* And what was that activity? That period of activity was all: *"God created and made,"* up to that period of time.

The *"created,"* (*bârâ'*), part; includes the creation of the heavens and the earth, man; as well as some other action that will be addressed shortly.

The *"made,"* (*'âsâh*), part; refers to actions God undertook other than literal creation.

And finally, verse 4 tells us: *"These are the generations of the heavens and of the earth when they were created, in the day that the Lord God made the earth and the heavens."* Here *"created"* is: *"bârâ';"*[19] and *"made"* is: *"'âsâh."*[20]

The actual Hebrew word translated as "generations" is:

> "8435 tôwl^{e}dâh; or tôl^{e}dâh; from 3205; (plur. only) *descent*, i.e. *family*; (fig.) *history*: - birth, generations."[21]

Contextually, it seems that the *figurative* meaning of *tôwl^{e}dâh* as *history*, is what is meant here. Thus these are the history(ies) *"of the heavens and of the earth when they were created,"* seems to be the most reasonable meaning. And when was this history *provided*? This is or was provided: *"in the day that the Lord God made the earth and the heavens."* Here the *"made"* refers to actions other than creation.

To the likely surprise of many, God did not actually do all that much actual creating in Genesis 1. In fact the word *bârâ'* appears only five times in Genesis 1. The creation of the heavens and the earth is the *first* appearance. The creation of man is the *second*, *third*, and *fourth* appearance.

And the final appearance of *bârâ'* is in Genesis 1:21 (KJV):

> *"And God created great whales,*
> *and every living creature that moveth,*
> *which the waters brought forth abundantly,*
> *after their kind, and every*
> *winged fowl after his kind:*
> *and God saw that it was good."*[22]

The True Purpose of Man

Thus up until the beginning of these Genesis 2 passages, all other actions taken by God could reasonably be placed in the "made;" or "6213 'âsâh; a prim. root; to do or make, in the broadest sense and widest application..." category.

And what about the *second* half of Genesis 2:1: "*and all the host of them?*" In context, again this is: "*Thus the heavens and the earth were finished, and all the host of them.*"

The actual word translated as "host" is:

"6635 tsâbâ' or ts^{e}bâ'âh from 6633; a *mass* of persons (or fig. things), espec. reg. organized for war (an *army*); by impl. a *campaign*, lit. or fig. (spec. *hardship*, *worship*): -appointed time, (+) army, (+) battle, company, host, service, soldiers, waiting upon, war (fare)."[23]

It is God *Himself* who is referring to created man as: "a *mass* of persons (or fig. things), espec. reg. organized for war (an *army*)."

This term *tsâbâ'* is perfectly consistent with God's expressed *desire* as stated in Genesis 1:26, to give man "*dominion*," or *râdâh*, "*over the earth*;" and the instructions God gave man in Genesis 1:28: to "*subdue*" or: "kâbash; a prim. root; to *tread* down; hence neg. to *disregard*; pos. to *conquer*, *subjugate*, *violate*: - bring into bondage, force, keep under, subdue, bring into subjection;" the earth.

Tsâbâ' is seen elsewhere in the Bible.

Numbers 2:3-4 (KJV) tell us:

"*And on the east side toward the rising*

The True Purpose of Man

*of the sun shall they of the standard
of the camp of Judah pitch throughout
their armies: and Nahshon
the son of Amminadab
shall be captain of the children of Judah.*

*And his host, and those that
were numbered of them,
were threescore and fourteen
thousand and six hundred.*"[24]

Here in Numbers, the word translated as "*armies*" and "*host,*" is *tsâbâ'*. Originally, the translation of *tsâbâ'* in verse 3 was also "host."[25]

2 Samuel 10:6-7 (KJV) tells us:

*"And when the children of Ammon
saw that they stank before David,
the children of Ammon sent and hired the
Syrians of Bethrehob and the Syrians of Zoba,
twenty thousand footmen,
and of king Maacah a thousand men,
and of Ishtob twelve thousand men.*

*And when David heard of it, he sent Joab,
and all the host of the mighty men.*"[26]

Here in 2 Samuel, the word translated as "*host,*" is *tsâbâ'*.[27]

As can easily be seen, the: "*the heavens and the earth were finished,*" in no way refers to the *condition* of the earth—else why did God create *tsâbâ'*, and then instruct these *tsâbâ'* to *kâbash* the earth? God's

The True Purpose of Man

role *in this particular matter* was finished, but it was the job of *tsâbâ'* to continue the process.

Earlier, Genesis 1:28 was cited as God's instruction to man: *"And God blessed them, and God said unto them, Be fruitful, and multiply, and replenish the earth, and subdue it: and have dominion over the fish of the sea, and over the fowl of the air, and over every living thing that moveth upon the earth."*

And again, the *"subdue it"* part is: "kâbash; a prim. root; to *tread* down; hence neg. to *disregard*; pos. to *conquer, subjugate, violate*: - bring into bondage, force, keep under, subdue, bring into subjection." And again the English word *kibosh* is derived from *kâbash*.

And although man translates what God Himself called man as "*host*;" the actual word provided by Moses, (assuming *Mosaic* authorship of Genesis), again is: "6635 tsâbâ' or ts^{e}bâ'âh from 6633; a *mass* of persons (or fig. things), espec. reg. organized for war (an *army*)."

So we are told that it is the purpose of man acting as *tsâbâ'*, or: "a *mass* of persons (or fig. things), espec. reg. organized for war;" to kâbash, or: "to *tread* down... to *conquer, subjugate, violate*" the earth—at least according to what God said.

But these are very *general* instructions, much more like the *goal* of or for mankind; rather than "host specific," which is the case with *objectives*. *Objectives* are considered as *SMART*; with this acronym here meaning: Specific, Measurable, Achievable, Realistic, and Time sensitive.

Thus although here God told us the purpose of mankind in the *general* sense; precisely what the

The True Purpose of Man

purpose of each *individual* should ideally be, cannot be derived from these words. Neither are we told here precisely *how*; i.e.; *by what means*, we are each to play our unique roles.

Ephesians 6:17 tells us:

> *"And take the helmet of salvation,
> and the sword of the Spirit,
> which is the word of God:"*[28]

[Following is an excerpt from "*Wisdom Essentials – It's Not Just A Theory.*"]

Tucked in at the very end of the list of defensive, (increasing resistance), measures in the preceding verses, and ending here in verse 17 after the last "*and;*" something rather interesting appears. In fact; therein lies a "bomb." And it is a rather interesting and quite powerful "bomb"—the same representing the provision of a key instruction: *"(take) the sword of the Spirit, which is the word of God."*

This instruction is the only *offensive* (voltage lowering) instruction given in these verses.

What does *"(take) the sword of the Spirit, which is the word of God"* mean?

The actual original Greek word translated as "sword" is:

> "*3162* machaira; prob. fem. of a presumed der. of *3163*; a *knife*, i.e. *dirk*; fig. *war, judicial punishment*: - sword."[WE25]

The True Purpose of Man

As can be seen, the translation as "*sword*" is misleading. A dirk is not a sword. "Knife" or "Dagger" would be a better translation. These are designed for "up close and personal" combat. This is important because this, (close up and tailor made); is precisely how the enemy attacks.

The figurative meaning should also be noted, that of "judicial punishment." There is an old saying: "Don't stick your head in the boxing ring if you don't want to get punched." It is the enemy who chooses to institute an attack. If the result is encountering a counterattack with a dirk, and he/it leaves a bit "bloodied," then he or it deserved it. But this should never be combined with anything that is of the enemy such as anger, hatred, etc. It is *justice*; ("judicial punishment"), and not *vengeance* that should be sought. If that which is of the enemy is at any time utilized, this can then easily be utilized by the enemy as a foothold.

The actual Greek word translated as "spirit" is:

> "*4151* pněuma; from *4154*; a *current* of air, i.e. *breath* (*blast*) or a *breeze*; by anal. or fig. a *spirit*, i.e. (human) the rational *soul*, (by impl.) *vital principle*, mental *disposition* etc..."[WE26]

Thus; "the knife of the soul" is a better translation. And precisely what is this "knife of the soul?"

It is the "word of God." What is this word? The actual Greek "word" translated here as "word" is:

The True Purpose of Man

"4487 rhēma; from 4483; an *utterance* (individ., collect. or spec.); by impl. a *matter* or *topic* (espec. of narration, command or dispute); with a neg. *naught* whatever..."[WE27]

John 1:1 tells us:

> "*In the beginning was the Word, and the Word was with God, and the Word was God.*"[WE28]

However the actual word translated here three times as "Word" is not rhēma, but rather:

"3056 lŏgŏs; from 3004; something *said* (including the *thought*); by impl. a *topic* (subject of discourse), also *reasoning* (the mental faculty) or *motive*; by extens. a *computation*; spec. (with the art. In John) the Divine *Expression* (i.e. *Christ*)"[WE29]

So it must be asked what is the difference between *rhēma* and *lŏgŏs*; and why was *rhēma* used by Paul, and *lŏgŏs* used in John?

Paul was giving instructions for *future* behavior, and John was recollecting *past* events. Thus *rhēma*; meaning an *utterance*; refers to what God *is* or *will be* saying "real time." *Lŏgŏs* refers to what God *has* or *had already* said."[29]

If one goes to the *lŏgŏs*, or the written word of God; and then also receives *rhēma*, or the "real time" "utterance" word of God; this is often referred to as *Bibliomancy*.

The True Purpose of Man

How is it that God provides this *rhēma*? Does He actually speak out loud? Not usually—although He has on occasion. God is usually much more subtle than this.

God will provide *rhēma* in a variety of ways: "I just had an idea." "I just had a feeling." "Something just told me to." "Somehow I just knew;" are all examples of the acknowledgement of the *actual* receipt of *rhēma*—whether this is *realized* or not.

There exists some basic or foundational *lŏgŏs*, originally presented as *rhēma*; and these are generally referred to as: "The Commandments." This is a bit of a misnomer, as God never actually "commanded" us to obey them—at least when they appear in Exodus 20. Instead, he asked us to do what is generally translated as "keep" them.

When God the Father spoke about "keeping" His "Commandments," the original Hebrew word is:

> "8104: shâmar; A prim. root; prop. to *hedge* about (as with thorns), i.e. *guard*; gen. to *protect*, *attend to*, etc.: - beware, be circumspect, take heed (to self), keep (-er, self), mark, look narrowly, observe, preserve, regard, reserve, save (self), sure, (that lay) wait (for), watch (-man)."[30]

And when Jesus spoke about "keeping" his "Commandments," the original Greek word is:

> "5083 tērĕō; from tĕrŏs (a *watch*; perh. akin to 2334); to *guard* (from *loss* or *injury*, prop. by keeping *the eye* upon..."[31]

The True Purpose of Man

Thus the "Commandments" are actually *informational* in nature; and not meant to represent an actual "command," in the sense of *requiring* obedience—at least according to the words chosen by God the Father, and Jesus.

The free will of man is so important, that even God himself would not interfere with man's decision to obey or not obey these commandments; but only "requires" that we *shâmar* or *tērĕō* the information; and then use this information in the decision making process. But these "Commandments" are the same for all, no matter what specific role any given host was designed to play.

Why is it that man should choose to obey these "Commandments?" The answer depends upon precisely what it is that one wants to subsequently reap. "Sowing" and "reaping" are not separate actualities. Whatever one chooses to "sow," represents a part of one actuality; with the ultimate and unavoidable "reaping," representing the other part of this *very same actuality*, resulting in balance.

Putting the *kibosh*, on the earth; or as God actually stated in Genesis 1:28 via the Hebrew *kâbash*; is again very broad, or *goal* oriented. Again, although most Bible "experts" would agree that the Bible is a "book about redemption;" they do *not* agree that it is the redemption of the earth to which this; "book about redemption" characterization refers. They do not understand that the original *created* hosts were brought into existence to *kâbash* the *earth*; and then much later the *formation* of the man known as Adam was the first act in the redemption of the *hosts*—to redeem the redeemers.

The True Purpose of Man

It is a "pretty tough sell," to suggest that the fruits of God's efforts as stated in Genesis 1:27: *"So God created man in his own image, in the image of God created he him; male and female created he them;"* required redemption from the "get go." It was because of the *contamination* of the *created* hosts from contact with the enemy while knowingly or unknowingly engaged in the *kâbash* process; that necessitated the beginning of the redemptive process for man. This process began with the *formation* of the "first Adam;" and was "finished" by the "last Adam."

One may argue that the formation of the first Adam took way too long, as this event occurred less than ten thousand years ago. But God has to play by the rules, and is subject to delay by man's errors. Thus the *kŏlpŏs*, or Bosom of Abraham, or Limbus Patrum, (the: "air conditioned section of hell"); was established for those who physically died prior to the availability of salvation.

But *redeem* and *subdue* are not necessarily the same. To simply *"subdue,"* "put the kibosh on," or *kâbash*; does not necessarily mean redemption. These very same acts could be evil, wicked, or both. Whether or not it is a redemptive act; depends upon other factors.

Each human being is and was designed and brought into existence with specific tasks in mind. One way to find out what these are; is the above *lŏgŏs*, or the written word of God; and *rhēma*. These are largely *informational* in nature.

At the time of that which is commonly known as: "The Last Supper," arguably: "The Last Seder," for

The True Purpose of Man

Christians; Jesus said something very interesting. And this statement is the subject of controversy even today.

John 14:12 (KJV) tells us:

> *"Verily, verily, I say unto you,*
> *He that believeth on me,*
> *the works that I do shall he do also;*
> *and greater works than these shall he*
> *do; because I go unto my Father."*[32]

The actual Greek word translated as "works" both times is:

> "2041 ĕrgŏn; from a prim. (but obsol.) ĕrgō (to *work*); *toil* (as an effort or occupation); by impl. an *act*: - deed, doing, labour, work."[33]

The original Greek word translated here as "greater" is:

> "3187 měizōn; irreg. compar. of 3173; *larger* (lit. or fig., spec. in age): - elder, greater (-est), more."[34]

Here "*works*" used in this context, is generally considered to represent the *results* or *fruits*. But the above definition of *ĕrgŏn* is unclear, as to whether this also represents the action of *working* as well.

But either way, we are being told that *if* the conditions of this statement are met; *then* greater or *měizōn* results than even those that Jesus achieved can be accomplished, after He went to the "Father."

The True Purpose of Man

If *ĕrgŏn* is translated as "*works*" is considered a *noun*; then greater *results* are possible. If *ĕrgŏn* is translated as "*works*" is considered a *verb*; then greater *means* are possible.

This passage is silent about the "type of means," and thus the "type of results;" to which this passage refers. Here "type of," refers to whether or not the *means* and/or *results* are consistent with, or inconsistent with natural law.

There are two types of *power* or *means* available in the universe:

dynamikós: (G) natural power, "from Greek *dynamikós* powerful, from *dynamis* power, from *dynasthai* be able, have power;"[35]

dunamis: (G) supernatural power "*1411 dunamis*; from *1410*; *force* (lit. or fig.); spec. miraculous *power* (usually by impl. a *miracle* itself)..."[36]

So it must be asked precisely which power it is to which Jesus is referring that will result in "*greater*," or *mĕizōn*; "*works*," or *ĕrgŏn*? Is it *dynamikós*, or *natural* power, that will result in greater *natural* results; or is it *dunamis*, or *supernatural* power, that will result in greater *supernatural* results, (miracles); to which Jesus is referring?

Before this is addressed, the enemy has been quite busy trying to change the meaning of this passage. This alone should reveal which power it is to which Jesus is referring. There are two main methods by

The True Purpose of Man

which the enemy has been attempting to change the meaning of this passage:

The *first* way, is the: "Apostolic Era Only" view of *dunamis*, or supernatural (miraculous) power. Here it is proffered that *dunamis* was available in this "Apostolic Era," but is no longer available today. There is no scriptural basis for this "view." But it is much easier for those who have no *dunamis*, to blame it on *unavailability*, rather than their *inability*—and this display of hubris pleases the enemy greatly.

And the *second* way, is to tacitly insert the words: "number of," or: "numbers of;" in between *měizōn* and *ěrgŏn*. So: "greater number of works," or: "greater numbers of works;" becomes the new translation. The "rationale" for this, is that since there are more Christians today; then a greater number of works is or are possible. Of course this is nonsense, as *měizōn* is adjectivally describing *ěrgŏn*; and the word number does not appear anywhere in the passage. And it is unclear if this "view" includes *dunamis*; or refers to *dynamikós* only.

Jesus was known for His *supernatural* or *dunamic* abilities, among many other things; rather than any *natural* or *dynamic* abilities. And contextually, *dunamis* fits quite well; while *dynamikós* would not.

But to understand *dunamis*, it must first be understood that it does not occur alone—even if its counterpart occurs *before* or *after* the *dunamis*.

In order to understand the Greek *dunamis*, the examination of a certain Hebrew word would be beneficial:

> "4853 *massâ'* from 5375; a burden; spec. tribute, or (abstr.) porterage; fig. an utterance, chiefly a doom, espec. singing; mental desire: - burden, carry away, prophesy..."[37]

Here with the Hebrew *massâ'*, it can be seen that translations of *massâ'* can be "prophesy" or "burden;" i.e.; supernatural power; or *personal*, or *subjective* "weight." This is because they always come together as a unit, even if there is a time lag. Here the Hebrew word *massâ'*, represents both, and as can be seen, is translated either way.

So what is it that is this counterpart of *dunamis*? The answer of course is *talent*—but not *talent* as commonly understood.

As *commonly* understood, *talent* might even be the very *dunamis* itself. Someone who has *talent*, usually has some type of capabilities in excess of those commonly seen. These unusual capabilities may be *dunamic* in nature; but are often called either *talent*, or *a gift*. With respect to the subject under discussion however; these capabilities are in fact neither *talent*, nor *a gift*.

Although a detailed analysis of this is beyond the scope of this work; the: "Talent Man Story," (actually a parable); is the explanation of the relationship between *talent* and *dunamis*. [See Chapter 10, "*True Talent*," contained in: "*Alleged Fantasy, Volume I Foundations*;" for this detailed analysis.]

So what is this *talent*? Many believe that a *talent* is a Hebrew unit of measure, ranging from 80 to 120 pounds, depending upon whether *common* or *royal*.

The True Purpose of Man

But the truth is that *talent* actually is from the Greek:

> "5007 talantŏn; neut. of a presumed der. of the orig. form of tiaō (to *bear*; equiv. to 5342); a *balance* (as *supporting* weights), i.e. (by impl.) a certain *weight* (and thence a *coin* or rather *sum* of money) or "*talent*": - talent."[38]

> "5342 phěrō; a prim. verb... to "*bear*" or carry."[39]

As can be seen, *talantŏn*; and its equivalent *phěrō*; are concerned with *subjective* weight; and the actions: "bear," "carry," and "balance." Thus it is the *effect* of this weight upon the one bearing or carrying this weight; and not the actual *objective* weight with which *talantŏn* is concerned.

The *implied* definition of *talantŏn* as: "a certain *weight* (and thence a *coin* or rather *sum* of money)," refers to the *reliability* of the amount of weight; and not any particular *objective* amount of weight.

In the aforementioned "Talent Man" parable, each was given *talantŏn* in accordance with the amount of *dunamis*, (not *dynamikós*), they each possessed. Two of the three worked, (put ergs into), their *talantŏn*; and received more. One buried his talent, and it was taken from him. This parable describes a *process*.

Unlike *lŏgŏs*, or the written word of God; or *rhēma*, or the "real time" word of God, which are largely *informational*; *talantŏn* is more *emotional* in nature. But it is not *emotional* in the usual sense.

The True Purpose of Man

A distinction must be made here between *feelings* and *emotions*. For these discussions, *feelings* represent the acquisition of information without the use of normal five senses. "I just knew I should," and "Something just told me to;" would thus be reasonably equivalent by this definition of *feelings*.

But *emotions* are entirely different. *Emotion* contains the root "motion;" thus implying an *imbalanced* state. How is this imbalanced state balanced? The answer is motion; with "move out" representing a fair definition of *e-motion*.

A *talantŏn* is an emotional imbalance that is caused by God, in furtherance of a specific reaction, by a specific host; to do some specific thing God wants done; i.e.; *motivation* to do some-thing. Unlike "normal" emotions, a *talantŏn* will not dissipate in the short term; although a *talantŏn* can be "buried;" i.e.; ignored and will eventually dissipate.

And also unlike most "normal" emotions, with a *talantŏn*; one will have "no peace" unless and until there is appropriate motion. And again, the *talantŏn* is the other side of the actuality known as *dunamis*. In Hebrew one word, massâ', describes the phenomenon—both the *supernatural* power, *and* the *burden* or *weight*. But in Greek, there are two words required to describe this phenomenon: *dunamis* for the supernatural power part; and *talantŏn* for the burden, or (balancing) weight.

How does one distinguish *dunamis*, from *dynamikós*? If it is a certainty; or perhaps better stated that to the extent that it is a certainty that any

The True Purpose of Man

natural law was violated, then it is with this same degree of certainty, by definition *dunamis*.

And the reasonable read, is that Jesus Himself told us that if one meets the conditions in His statement, then that person would be capable of greater works than even Jesus did.

But as the "Talent Man" story tells us, this is a *process*. And every process must begin at some point. Where does this process begin for each of us?

Romans 12:3 (KJV) tells us:

> *"For I say, through the grace
> given unto me,
> to every man that is among you,
> not to think of himself more
> highly than he ought to think;
> but to think soberly,
> according as God hath dealt
> to every man the measure of faith."*[40]

[Following is an excerpt from *"Alleged Fantasy Volume I - Foundations."*]

Precisely what is this: *"dealt to every man the measure of faith?"* Meaning, since this is proffered as the reason why one should not: "think more highly than he ought to think" about himself; precisely what is this that is under discussion.

One answer to this is "seed *ĕxŏusia*," or baseline *dunamic* power and *authority*. This is the granting of say "one talent," in the hope of a host working this *talantŏn*; and obtaining at least one *duna* of *dunamis* in return."[41]

The True Purpose of Man

Here the word *"faith"* is *pistis*,[42] meaning "persuade" or "convince."[43] How is this done?

One way is to "see the system work," as explained in the "Talent Man" parable. Work the *talantŏn*, and get the *dunamis*; and then do it again when the next *talantŏn* arrives.

Another way is by the demonstration of this *dunamis* to others. The latter is precisely what Jesus did. Unbeknownst to most; many, (but not all), of the miracles performed by Jesus had been performed by others in the past. In addition to fulfilling the Biblical prophesy, this was done to remind people of their capabilities. In fact, it could be reasonably argued that providing this reminder was the very purpose for some of that which was included in these particular prophesies.

Rhēma and *lŏgŏs* are largely *informational*; but either can lead to the acquisition of *dunamis*. And it is the application of *ergs* into the system, which will increase the *dunamic* capabilities. The *talantŏn* provides the "drive," or the "insatiable" desire to move; and the application of ergs ultimately results in increased levels of *dunamis*. And this cycle can be repeated until: *"greater works than," "the works that I do," "shall he do."* And since Jesus already went: *"unto my Father;"* this power is available right now to any: *"He that believeth on me, the works that I do."*

Any host's acquisition of *dunamis*, or supernatural power, represents a serious *offensive* threat to the enemy. But the level of this *offensive* threat depends upon both the *level* of power acquired; and the *will* of the host. Thus the efficacy of this *"sword,"* or dirk; the *machaira* of the *pneuma*; is the result of the

The True Purpose of Man

understanding of, and the *acting upon* the Word of God.

The enemy not only does not want any host to obtain *dunamis*; but he does not want any host to even know *dunamis* is even obtainable. And should any host become aware of *dunamic* capabilities, and then obtain any level of the same; it is *will* that is then severely attacked.

Matthew 7:13-14 (KJV) tells us:

> *"Enter ye in at the strait gate:*
> *for wide is the gate, and broad is the way,*
> *that leadeth to destruction,*
> *and many there be which go in thereat:*
>
> *Because strait is the gate,*
> *and narrow is the way,*
> *which leadeth unto life,*
> *and few there be that find it."*[44]

Most believe that Jesus is speaking here of salvation; i.e.; these are the same "gates," as the "gates" in the passages of Luke 13:23-25. However as will shortly be seen, this is not so.

Luke 13:23-25 (KJV) tells us:

> *"Then said one unto him, Lord,*
> *are there few that be saved?*
>
> *And he said unto them,*
> *Strive to enter in at the strait gate:*
> *for many, I say unto you, will seek to*
> *enter in, and shall not be able.*

The True Purpose of Man

> *When once the master of the house is*
> *risen up, and hath shut to the door,*
> *and ye begin to stand without, and to*
> *knock at the door, saying, Lord, Lord,*
> *open unto us; and he shall*
> *answer and say unto you,*
> *I know you not whence ye are:*"[45]

[Following is an Excerpt from "*Alleged Fantasy Volume I - Foundations.*"]

Here in *Luke*, it seems Jesus is clearly referring to salvation, as that was the subject of the inquiry to him: "*are there just a few who are being saved?*"

The original Greek word translated as "saved" in Luke 13:23 is:

> "4982 sōzō; from a prim. sōs (contr. for obsol. saŏs "*safe*"); to *save*, i.e. *deliver* or *protect* (lit. or fig.): - heal, preserve, save (self), do well, be (make) whole."[AF1]

The *context* of Jesus' answer to the *question;* is critical in understanding the meaning of these passages. The *question* had to do with *how many* are being saved: "*are there few that be saved?*"

Thus it seems reasonable that Jesus' *answer* would, at least in some way or manner, be concerned with this very same matter.

The actual Greek word translated as "strait" here in Luke 13:24: "*Strive to enter in at the strait gate,*" is:

> "4728 stěnŏs; prob, from the base of *2476*; *narrow* (from obstacles *standing* close about): - strait."[AF2]

Here there is a sense of "narrow" or a "strait," as it relates to the presence of *obstacles*. The common definition of *strait* is consistent with this, (see *stenosis*). But if "strait" is *spoken* instead of *read*, many would hear the word "straight," as in non-crooked, or the shortest distance between two points.

The *struggle*, has to do with whether few or many will obtain salvation by entering the "*strait*" door, or via Jesus himself; as He is the only "door" to salvation. In fact, today there are many more obstacles causing a narrowing or an even "straiter strait." Much of this additional narrowing, is the direct result of governmental actions—most particularly the courts."[46]

But again Matthew 7:13-14 (KJV) tells us:

> *"Enter ye in at the strait gate: for wide*
> *is the gate, and broad is the way,*
> *that leadeth to destruction,*
> *and many there be which go in thereat:*
>
> *Because strait is the gate,*
> *and narrow is the way,*
> *which leadeth unto life,*
> *and few there be that find it."*

The True Purpose of Man

Once again, most believe that here in Matthew 7:13-14, Jesus is also speaking of *salvation*, as He was in the above passages in Luke 13:23-25; however—

[Following is an Excerpt from "*Alleged Fantasy Volume I - Foundations.*"]

At this juncture, in order to provide proper *context* for Matthew 7:13-14 above, it would be appropriate, arguably *necessary*, to consider the verses being those which *directly precede* the above Matthew: 7:13-14, namely Matthew 7:7-12.

It becomes obvious that the topic Jesus is speaking about here in these preceding verses, Matthew 7:7-12, is not *salvation*, but rather aspects of our *behavior*.

Matthew 7:7-12 (KJV) tells us:

> *"Ask, and it shall be given you;*
> *seek, and ye shall find; knock,*
> *and it shall be opened unto you:*
>
> *For every one that asketh receiveth;*
> *and he that seeketh findeth;*
> *and to him that knocketh*
> *it shall be opened.*
> *Or what man is there of you,*
> *whom if his son ask bread,*
> *will he give him a stone?*
>
> *Or if he ask a fish,*
> *will he give him a serpent?*
> *If ye then, being evil,*

> *know how to give good gifts*
> *unto your children,*
> *how much more shall your Father*
> *which is in heaven give good*
> *things to them that ask him?*
>
> *Therefore all things whatsoever*
> *ye would that men should do to you,*
> *do ye even so to them: for this*
> *is the law and the prophets.*"[AF3]

Firstly, it must be determined precisely what the meaning of the two "its" are in verse 7: "*Ask, and it shall be given you,*" and: "*knock, and it shall be opened unto you;*" as well as the meaning of the singular "it" in verse 8: "*to him that knocketh it shall be opened;*"—respectively.

The *second* "it" in verse 7, ("*knock, and it shall be opened unto you*"); sounds suspiciously like the *salvation* door in Luke, which will be closed at some point in time.

But the *first* "it" in verse 7, ("*Ask, and it shall be given you*"); reads a bit differently. Here the "it" is something that will be given, and given in accord with whatever it was that was "asked for."

Thus it seems that in order for this particular, (the *first*), "it" to be limited to something related to a *door*; it seems one would to have had to have *asked* for a door—assuming the "*knock,*" "*knocketh,*" and "*opened;*" refer to actions taken upon a door.

The "*it*" in verse 8, ("*and to him that knocketh it shall be opened*"); is provided as part of an *explanation* of some type of principle, as we are told:

"For (because) every one that asketh receiveth; and he that seeketh findeth;" appearing just before: *"and to him that knocketh it shall be opened."*

There are then some examples cited, and we are then provided with the conclusion beginning with a *"therefore;"* or what an attorney might phrase as: "For all of the foregoing reasons: *"Therefore*; ("For all of the foregoing reasons"); *all things whatsoever ye would that men should do to you, do ye even so to them: for this is the law and the prophets."*

This is Jesus explaining what is contemporarily referred to as the law of *karma*, or law *compensation*—no matter how angry some "Christian folk" may become by associating *Jesus'* teachings, with a word of *Buddhist* origin.

…Jesus concludes the subject of these passages with: *"for this is the law and the prophets."*[47]

After concluding these subjects, Jesus then begins speaking about an entirely different subject in the very next verses, the verses under analysis: Matthew 7:13-14.

Again, most believe this subject to be *salvation* in Matthew 7:13-14, just as in Luke 13:23-25; but careful analysis proves this is not so.

Here again is Matthew 7:13-14 (KJV): *"Enter ye in at the strait gate: for wide is the gate, and broad is the way, that leadeth to destruction, and many there be which go in thereat: Because strait is the gate, and narrow is the way, which leadeth unto life, and few there be that find it."*

[Following is an excerpt from *"Alleged Fantasy Volume I - Foundations."*]

The True Purpose of Man

The actual Greek word translated as "strait" in "*strait gate*" here in Matthew 7:13 is also *stĕnŏs*.[AF4]

The actual Greek word translated as "gate," is as was seen previously in Luke:

> "4439 pulē; appar. a prim. word; a *gate*, i.e. the leaf or wing of a folding *entrance* (lit. or fig.): - gate."[AF5]

The actual Greek word translated as "wide," is:

> "4116 platus; from *4111*; spread out *"flat"* ("plot"), i.e. *broad*: - wide."[AF6]

The actual Greek word translated as "broad," is:

> "2149 ĕuruchōrŏs; from ĕurus (*wide*) and 5561; *spacious*: - broad."[AF7]

The actual Greek word translated as "strait," (strait gate) in Matthew 17:14 is again *stĕnŏs*.[AF8]

However; the actual Greek word translated as "*narrow* ("*narrow* way") here in Matthew 7:14 is not *stĕnŏs*, but rather:

> "2346 thlibō; akin to the base of *5147*; to crowd (lit. or fig.): - afflict, narrow, throng, suffer tribulation, trouble."[AF9]

> "5147 tribŏs; from tribō (to "rub"; akin to tĕirō, truō, and the base of 5131, 5134); a rut or worn track: - path"[AF10]

The True Purpose of Man

The actual Greek word translated as "destruction" is:

> "684 apōlĕia; from a presumed der. of 622; *ruin* or *loss* (phys., spiritual or eternal): - damnable (- nation), destruction, die, perdition, x perish, pernicious ways, waste."[AF11]

> "622 apŏllumi; from 575 and the base of 3639 to *destroy* fully (reflex. to *perish*, or *lose*), lit. or fig.: - destroy, die, lose, mar, perish."[AF12]

And according to Strong, the *only* time the word *apōlĕia* is ever translated as *destruction* in the entire four gospels, (MMLJ), is in this (Matthew 7:13 KJV), passage.[AF13]

In another unrelated chapter of Matthew, (Matthew 26:8 KJV); when the woman pours the expensive ointment or perfume on Jesus' head, the disciples asked: *"'To what purpose is this waste?'"*[AF14] The actual word translated in this passage as "waste," is also *apōlĕia*.[AF15]

Likewise in Mark, (Mark 14:4, KJV); when recounting the same story, the word *apōlĕia* is also translated as "waste" in: *"'Why was this waste of the ointment made?'"*[AF16]

Thus, it seems that "ruin, loss or waste" represents a better definition or translation of the original Greek word *apōlĕia*, than would be *destruction* or *death*.

However, one problem with this position; is that there is at least an implied comparison between the

The True Purpose of Man

translation of *apōlĕia* as destruction or death; because at least at this juncture, it seems that Jesus indicated that those who find this other gate will find life, instead of destruction or death. So because of this, it might also seem fair to consider that the appropriate translation of *apōlĕia* would be as destruction or death; based upon this implied comparison of *apōlĕia* with life; with life being the *opposite* of destruction or death.

But then again, it must be asked that if *destruction* or *death*, instead of *waste*, were the correct meaning for what Jesus spoke in Aramaic; then why was it that the above "*apŏllumi*; "... to *destroy* fully (reflex. to *perish*, or *lose*), lit. or fig.: - destroy, die, lose, mar, perish," was not chosen as the most synonymic Greek word? Instead it was *apōlĕia*; albeit *derived* from *apŏllumi*; which was chosen as most synonymic.

Thus a fair translation of Matthew 17:13, based upon the original Greek would be: "*Enter* (ĕisĕrchŏmal) *ye in at the narrow from obstacles standing close about* (stĕnŏs) *gate: for 'spread out flat* (platus) *is the gate, and* (wide) *and spacious* (ĕuruchōrŏs) *is the "road,* (hŏdŏs) *that leadeth to waste ruin or loss,* (apōlĕia), *and many there be which go in thereat*"

There is no mention of *salvation*, either here in Matthew 17:13, or in the verses preceding it. So if it can be stipulated that Jesus was *not* speaking about *salvation* here Matthew 17:13, it must be asked precisely what it was of which He was in fact speaking?

The True Purpose of Man

There is the one gate or door that is *narrow* because of obstacles. At this juncture, it is unclear as to precisely what it is that is on the other side of this gate or door.

And there is another gate or door; that is a "spread out flat" gate; as well as a "wide and spacious" road leading to this "other gate."

But we are told precisely what is that is on the other side of this "other (wide) gate:" *apōlĕia* or *"waste ruin or loss."*

And we are also told, that with respect to this "other," or *apōlĕia*, gate or door: *"many there be which go in thereat."*

At this juncture; it can reasonably be inferred that if: *"many there be which go in thereat;"* with respect to this second, or "other" (the wide), gate or door; then likely "few" *"there be which go in thereat,"* with regard to the narrow door.

And the *conclusion* is contained in the very next verse, here again is Matthew 7:14 (KJV): *"Because strait is the gate, and narrow is the way, which leadeth unto life, and few there be that find it."*

Here in verse 14, we are told precisely *why* that which is contained in verse 13 is true, as verse 14 begins with the word: *"because."*

As previously cited, here the original Greek word for *"strait"* in describing this *"gate"* is again *stĕnŏs*; and the original Greek word translated as "gate" is again *pulē* But with regard to the *"way,"* the original Greek word for "narrow" here in describing the *"way"* is not *stĕnŏs*, but rather *thlibō*.

The True Purpose of Man

And we are now told what is on the other side of this particular (verse 14) gate, as *this* gate: *"leadeth unto life, and few there be that find it."*

Life means *connection*; and death means *disconnection*. There is *physical life* when the soul is connected to the physical body; and *physical death* when disconnected. There is *spiritual life* when the soul is connected to its original source, (God); and *spiritual death* when disconnected.

But it seems that *all* to whom these words were spoken, were already *physically* alive. So a fair question for Jesus' audience, would be: "Why should I mess with that *stěnŏs*, and all of those obstacles close by; when I am already 'alive?'" Or perhaps: "But I am already on the other side of this gate."

An alternative explanation would be that this "life," actually means: "spiritual life;" and so then it actually is *salvation*; just like in Luke; that Jesus was speaking of in these passages. But if this is stipulated as so, then Jesus would have simply "jumped into" this discussion completely out of context.

Thus we are faced with the choice of believing that Jesus was telling physically alive persons to enter this gate in order to attain physical life; or; that Jesus was referring to "spiritual life," just as in Luke; with *no additional knowledge* available to us in these passages. Or that Jesus was referring to "X."

The actual Greek word translated here as "life" is:

"2222 zōē; from *2198*; *life* (lit. or fig.): - life (-time). Comp. 5590."[AF17]

The True Purpose of Man

"2198 zaō; a prim. verb; to *live* (lit. or fig.): - life (-time), (a-) live (-ly), quick."[AF18]

"5590 psuchē; from 5594; *breath*, i.e. (by impl.) *spirit*, abstr. or concr. (the *animal* sentient principle only; thus distinguished on the one hand from 4151, which is the rational and immortal *soul*; and on the other from 2222 which is mere *vitality*, even of plants: these terms thus exactly correspond respectively to the Heb. 5315, 7307 and 2416): - heart (+- ily), life, mind, soul, + us, + you."[AF19]

"4151 pněuma; from 4154; a *current* of air, i.e. *breath* (*blast*) or a *breeze*; by anal. or fig. a *spirit*, i.e. (human) the rational *soul*, (by impl.) *vital principle*, mental *disposition*, etc., or (superhuman) an *angel*, *doemon*, or (divine) *God*, Christ's *spirit*, the Holy *Spirit*: - ghost, life, spirit(ual, ually), mind. Comp. 5590."[AF20]

Here in the definition of *psuchē*, as per Strong's suggested comparison of *zōē* with 5590 *psuchē*, distinctions are easily seen. Here it is "mere *vitality*, even of plants," which represents the definition of *zōē*, as appears in the definition of *psuchē*.

Neither the immaterial part of man as *psuchē*: "the *animal* sentient principle only;" nor the immaterial part of man as *pněuma*: "the rational and immortal *soul*;" is not only not included in the definition of

The True Purpose of Man

zōē, but each are specifically *excluded* from being in the definition of *zōē*—at least according to Strong.

Since it is only *pnĕuma*, and some may even argue *psuchē*; that is or are in need of *salvation*; and since it appears that each is *precluded* from being included in the definition of *zōē*; it could not have been *salvation*, (the *means* for attaining *spiritual* life), about which Jesus was speaking at that time, as per what is contained here in Matthew.

And since all that could hear Jesus at that time were already physically alive, it could not have been *physical* life about which, ("*leadeth to*") Jesus was speaking at that time."[48]

What Jesus was speaking about here, was the *apōlĕia*, or: "*waste ruin or loss*" of one's: "*zōē*; from 2198; *life* (lit. or fig.): - life (-time);" which is derived from "*zaō*; a prim. verb; to *live* (lit. or fig.)." This is what happens to one's "lifetime," if that "*gate*" which is "*wide*;" to which the "*way*" is "*broad*;" is chosen— the "*gate*" that: "*many there be which go in thereat.*"

This is not the "*waste ruin or loss*" of man's *physical* life. This is not the "*waste ruin or loss*" of man's *spiritual* life; i.e.; loss of salvation. This is the "*waste ruin or loss*" of man's "lifetime." Meaning; the *purpose* for man's lifetime as stated in Genesis 1:28, when man is instructed by God to *kâbash*; (In English: Put the kibosh on.); the earth; and man later being referred to by God as *tsâbâ'*: "a *mass* of persons (or fig. things), espec. reg. organized for war (an *army*)."

And of course this "*wide*" "*waste ruin or loss*" "*gate*" is "*wide*" because there are little or no *stěnŏs* because of obstacles placed there by the enemy. In

The True Purpose of Man

addition, the *"way"* to this *"gate"* is *"broad"* because there is no *thlibō*: "to crowd (lit. or fig.): - afflict, narrow, throng, suffer tribulation, trouble;" deliberately placed there to be "in the way."

These *stěnŏs*, or *"narrow* (from obstacles *standing* close about);" and these *thlibō*, or: "to crowd (lit. or fig.): - afflict, narrow, throng, suffer tribulation, trouble;" are all reserved for, and dedicated to; the gate where man's *zōē*, or "lifetime," will *not* be subject to: *"waste ruin or loss."*

It is that which *thlibō* or *crowds*, that man must overcome to get to that "lifetime" gate. That which is trying to prevent an individual from getting to this *zōē* gate, fears the results if any man should become one of the; *"few there be that find it."*

On the other side of this *"gate"* lie wisdom and power in quantities difficult to even imagine. And once one gets there, they become essentially unstoppable—at least while they are physically alive.

This *zōē* *"gate"* is custom made for each human being. There is a lock on this *"gate,"* that automatically opens once the person for whom it is custom designed gets to this *"gate."* The enemy, or those that *thlibō* or *crowds* the *"way;"* must stop the arrival by crowding, or *thlibō* the *"way;"* and/or by placing obstacles, or *stěnŏs*.

It is the inability to get through the crowding, and or the obstacles; that is the true reason for the "Apostolic Era Only" excuse for lack of *dunamis*.

The first *four* books of the New Testament: Matthew, Mark, Luke, and John, are about *Jesus*; or the *Second* Part of the Trinity. The *fifth* book of the New Testament, the book of "Acts;" is about the

The True Purpose of Man

Christ, or the *Third* Part of the Trinity. It is the power of the Holy Ghost that increases this ability to act—hence the name: "Book of Acts."

As one progressively overcomes the *crowding*, and the *obstacles* to this "*gate*;" there are increasing levels of the Holy Ghost being *on* him and *in* him. Once this "*gate*" is entered, the Holy Ghost is fully *in* Him. This is the "helper" promised by Jesus, who will provide the wisdom and power to perform "*works*" even "*greater*" than those done by Jesus.

And upon entering this "gate," structure and function become one. Meaning; that the unique design of that particular host by God to perform certain functions; and the capabilities to perform those same functions are "in synch."

This means the enemy must go to "Plan C."

"Plan A" was based upon maintaining the *ignorance* of the host. "Plan B" was the *crowding* and the placement of *obstacles*. These two "Plans," are much easier for the enemy; as there is much specificity; and there is always that "*wide*" gate, and that "*broad*" way; as a diversion to get a host to: "take the easy way in."

But once the *zōē*, or "lifetime" gate is reached, everything changes. Now the enemy is forced to fight that which represents essentially incalculable amounts of wisdom and power; and most importantly *unpredictability*.

"So then should I find a religion?"

No, not necessarily; as that may be the worst thing that can be done. There are some religions that might be helpful in this regard; however most major religions have become "Pseudo-Statist" enterprises.

[See: "*Statists Saving One*," Chapter 10: "*The Pseudo Statists*."] These are largely concerned with the accumulation of wealth; and the regulation of behaviors to *their* liking—irrespective of whether said behaviors are to *God's* liking, or are even consistent with His Word in any meaningful way.

And another problem, is that the mummery and flummery often present; whether by design or otherwise; tend to provide just enough to satiate the *talantŏn* or drive, to a level just below the: "action required" level.

"The more modern versions of the Bible are best—Right?"

No, most if not all Bible versions are just that: *versions*, and not *translations*. Many simply build upon the errors of others. This will most certainly interfere with the *lŏgŏs*; and thus may make the *rhēma* more difficult. Strong's is keyed to the KJV, but the KJV is also flawed. The *earlier* NAS Bibles claim to be as accurate as possible, and appear to be so. And the original 1890 Strong's is the best, irrespective of the year of printing.

"What is the most important thing I can do right now?

Go to the *lŏgŏs*, seeking *rhēma*; and "rightly divide", (see two), the Word of God.

But above all—Get moving!

"The True Purpose of Man," is a member of the MeekRaker family of publications—"Non-Secular Publications That Make Sense."

Visit us at MeekRaker.com

Bibliography

1. *King James Bible*, Genesis 1:1
2. Strong, James. *Strong's Exhaustive Concordance of the Bible*. ©1890 James Strong, Madison, NJ p. 106 (Hebrew)
3. Strong, James. *Strong's Exhaustive Concordance of the Bible*. ©1890 James Strong, Madison, NJ p. 23 (Hebrew)
4. *Holy Bible Saint Joseph New Catholic Edition*. ©1962, ©1957-1949 Catholic Book Publishing Co., NY. p.15
5. *King James Bible*, Genesis 1:2
6. *Interlinear Bible Hebrew Greek English, 1 Volume edition*. © 1976, 1977, 1978, 1979, 1980, 1981, 1984. Second Edition, © 1986 Jay P. Green, Sr., Hendrickson Publishers (Genesis 1:2) p. 1
7. *King James Bible*, Genesis 1:26
8. *King James Bible*, Genesis 1:27
9. Strong, James. *Strong's Exhaustive Concordance of the Bible*. ©1890 James Strong, Madison, NJ p. 107 (Hebrew)
10. Strong, James. *Strong's Exhaustive Concordance of the Bible*. ©1890 James Strong, Madison, NJ p. 225
11. *King James Bible*, Genesis 1:28
12. Strong, James. *Strong's Exhaustive Concordance of the Bible*. ©1890 James Strong, Madison, NJ p. 54 (Hebrew)
13. *King James Bible*, Genesis 2:1
14. Strong, James. *Strong's Exhaustive Concordance of the Bible*. ©1890 James Strong, Madison, NJ p. 55 (Hebrew)
15. *King James Bible*, Genesis 2:2-4
16. Strong, James. *Strong's Exhaustive Concordance of the Bible*. ©1890 James Strong, Madison, NJ p. 92 (Hebrew)

The True Purpose of Man

17. Strong, James. *Strong's Exhaustive Concordance of the Bible.* ©1890 James Strong, Madison, NJ p. 225
18. Strong, James. *Strong's Exhaustive Concordance of the Bible.* ©1890 James Strong, Madison, NJ p. 48 (Hebrew)
19. Strong, James. *Strong's Exhaustive Concordance of the Bible.* ©1890 James Strong, Madison, NJ p. 225
20. Strong, James. *Strong's Exhaustive Concordance of the Bible.* ©1890 James Strong, Madison, NJ p. 640
21. Strong, James. *Strong's Exhaustive Concordance of the Bible.* ©1890 James Strong, Madison, NJ p. 119 (Hebrew)
22. *King James Bible*, Genesis 1:21
23. Strong, James. *Strong's Exhaustive Concordance of the Bible.* ©1890 James Strong, Madison, NJ p. 98 (Hebrew)
24. *King James Bible*, Numbers 2:3-4
25. Strong, James. *Strong's Exhaustive Concordance of the Bible.* ©1890 James Strong, Madison, NJ p. 492
26. *King James Bible*, 2 Samuel 10:6-7
27. Strong, James. *Strong's Exhaustive Concordance of the Bible.* ©1890 James Strong, Madison, NJ p. 493
28. *King James Bible*, Ephesians 6:17
29. Walker, J. Bartholomew. Wisdom Essentials ©2017 Quadrakoff Publications Group, LLC Wilmington DE pp. 58-61
30. Strong, James. *Strong's Exhaustive Concordance of the Bible.* ©1890 James Strong, Madison, NJ p. 118 (Hebrew)
31. Strong, James. *Strong's Exhaustive Concordance of the Bible.* ©1890 James Strong, Madison, NJ p. 71 (Greek)
32. *King James Bible*, John 14:12
33. Strong, James. *Strong's Exhaustive Concordance of the Bible.* ©1890 James Strong, Madison, NJ p. 32 (Greek)
34. Strong, James. *Strong's Exhaustive Concordance of the Bible.* ©1890 James Strong, Madison, NJ p. 47 (Greek)
35. *Chambers Dictionary of Etymology*, Copyright ©1988 The H. W. Wilson Company, New York, NY p. 308

Bibliography

36. Strong, James. *Strong's Exhaustive Concordance of the Bible.* ©1890 James Strong, Madison, NJ p. 58 (Greek)
37. Strong, James. *Strong's Exhaustive Concordance of the Bible.* ©1890 James Strong, Madison, NJ p. 73 (Hebrew)
38. Strong, James. *Strong's Exhaustive Concordance of the Bible.* ©1890 James Strong, Madison, NJ p. 70 (Greek)
39. Strong, James. *Strong's Exhaustive Concordance of the Bible.* ©1890 James Strong, Madison, NJ p. 74 (Greek)
40. *King James Bible*, Romans 12:3
41. Walker/Quadrakoff. *Alleged Fantasy Volume I - Foundations.* ©2020 Quadrakoff Publications Group, LLC Wilmington DE pp. 382
42. Strong, James. *Strong's Exhaustive Concordance of the Bible.* ©1890 James Strong, Madison, NJ p. 330
43. Strong, James. *Strong's Exhaustive Concordance of the Bible.* ©1890 James Strong, Madison, NJ p. 58 (Greek)
44. *King James Bible*, Matthew 7:13-14
45. *King James Bible*, Luke 13:23-25
46. Walker/Quadrakoff. *Alleged Fantasy Volume I - Foundations.* ©2020 Quadrakoff Publications Group, LLC Wilmington DE pp. 87-88
47. Walker/Quadrakoff. *Alleged Fantasy Volume I - Foundations.* ©2020 Quadrakoff Publications Group, LLC Wilmington DE pp. 90-92
48. Walker/Quadrakoff. *Alleged Fantasy Volume I - Foundations.* ©2020 Quadrakoff Publications Group, LLC Wilmington DE pp. 93-98

Embedded Bibliography
(In Order of Occurrence)

WE25. Strong, James. *Strong's Exhaustive Concordance of the Bible.* © 1890 James Strong, Madison, NJ p. 46 (Greek)

WE26. Strong, James. *Strong's Exhaustive Concordance of the Bible.* © 1890 James Strong, Madison, NJ p. 58 (Greek)

The True Purpose of Man

WE27. Strong, James. *Strong's Exhaustive Concordance of the Bible.* © 1890 James Strong, Madison, NJ p. 63 (Greek)

WE28. *King James Bible,* Ephesians 6:17 John 1:1

WE29. Strong, James. *Strong's Exhaustive Concordance of the Bible.* © 1890 James Strong, Madison, NJ p. 45 (Greek)

AF1. Strong, James. *Strong's Exhaustive Concordance of the Bible.* © 1890 James Strong, Madison, NJ p. 70 (Greek)

AF2. Strong, James. *Strong's Exhaustive Concordance of the Bible.* © 1890 James Strong, Madison, NJ p. 69 (Greek)

AF3. *King James Bible,* Matthew 7:13-14

AF4. Strong, James. *Strong's Exhaustive Concordance of the Bible.* © 1890 James Strong, Madison, NJ p. 979

AF5. Strong, James. *Strong's Exhaustive Concordance of the Bible.* © 1890 James Strong, Madison, NJ p. 63 (Greek)

AF6. Strong, James. *Strong's Exhaustive Concordance of the Bible.* © 1890 James Strong, Madison, NJ p. 58 (Greek)

AF7. Strong, James. *Strong's Exhaustive Concordance of the Bible.* © 1890 James Strong, Madison, NJ p. 34 (Greek)

AF8. Strong, James. *Strong's Exhaustive Concordance of the Bible.* © 1890 James Strong, Madison, NJ p. 979

AF9. Strong, James. *Strong's Exhaustive Concordance of the Bible.* © 1890 James Strong, Madison, NJ p. 36 (Greek)

AF10. Strong, James. *Strong's Exhaustive Concordance of the Bible.* © 1890 James Strong, Madison, NJ p. 72 (Greek)

AF11. Strong, James. *Strong's Exhaustive Concordance of the Bible.* © 1890 James Strong, Madison, NJ p. 15 (Greek)

AF12. Strong, James. *Strong's Exhaustive Concordance of the Bible.* © 1890 James Strong, Madison, NJ p. 14 (Greek)

AF13. Strong, James. *Strong's Exhaustive Concordance of the Bible.* © 1890 James Strong, Madison, NJ p. 259

AF14. *King James Bible,* Matthew 26:18

AF15. Strong, James. *Strong's Exhaustive Concordance of the Bible.* © 1890 James Strong, Madison, NJ p. 1107

Bibliography

AF16. *King James Bible,* Mark 14:4

AF17. Strong, James. *Strong's Exhaustive Concordance of the Bible.* © 1890 James Strong, Madison, NJ p. 35 (Greek)

AF18. Strong, James. *Strong's Exhaustive Concordance of the Bible.* © 1890 James Strong, Madison, NJ p. 34 (Greek)

AF19. Strong, James. *Strong's Exhaustive Concordance of the Bible.* © 1890 James Strong, Madison, NJ p. 79 (Greek)

AF20. Strong, James. *Strong's Exhaustive Concordance of the Bible.* © 1890 James Strong, Madison, NJ p. 58 (Greek)

Sources
&
Suggested Reading

ALLEGED FANTASY VOLUME I – FOUNDATIONS

MEEKRAKER BEGINNINGS...

WISDOM ESSENTIALS—THE PENTALOGY

STATISTS SAVING ONE

OSTIUM AB INFERNO

REINCARNATION—
A REASONABLE INQUIRY

LEARNING HOW TO BE GAY

DONALD TRUMP CANDIDACY
ACCORDING TO MATTHEW?

SHÂMAR TO SHARIA

IT'S NOT JUST A THEORY

CALVARY'S HIDDEN TRUTHS

INEVITABLE BALANCE

QPG Publications are available
wherever you buy fine books.
MeekRaker.com

www.ingramcontent.com/pod-product-compliance
Lightning Source LLC
Chambersburg PA
CBHW030201100526
44592CB00009B/389